MW00805365

My Adam and Eve Book of OPPOSITES

Books in this Series

My Adam and Eve Book of Opposites
My Noah's Ark Book of Colors
My Baby Jesus Book of Numbers
My Bible Story Book of ABC's

Copyright © 1995 by Educational Publishing Concepts, Inc., Wheaton, Illinois

Published by Concordia Publishing House
3558 S. Jefferson Avenue, St. Louis, MO 63118-3968
Manufactured in the United States of America

All rights reserved. No part of this publication may be reproduced, stored in a retrieval system, or transmitted, in any form or by any means, electronic, mechanical, photocopying, recording, or otherwise, without the prior written permission of Concordia Publishing House.

1 2 3 4 5 6 7 8 9 10   04 03 02 01 00 99 98 97 96 95

My Adam and Eve Book of OPPOSITES

Glenda Palmer

Illustrated by
Rick Incrocci

CPH™
SAINT LOUIS

Where did our world come from?
Where did all the plants come from?
And where did all the animals come from?

God created them. He made them in only one week—seven days. God worked for six days. He rested on the seventh day. **Work** and **rest** are so different, they are called **opposites**.

On the first
day God created
light. He called
it **day**. He called
the **dark, night**.

Light is the opposite of **dark**. **Day** is the opposite of **night**.

On the second day, God made the sky **up above** and the earth **down below**. **Up** and **down** are opposites. **Above** and **below** are opposites too.

God separated the **wet** oceans from **dry** land on the third day. **Wet** is the opposite of **dry.**

Then God created the plants.
Tall trees and **short** grass.
Plain leaves and **fancy** flowers.

Thick trunks and **thin** stems.
Tall and **short**,
Plain and **fancy**,
Thick and **thin** are all opposites.

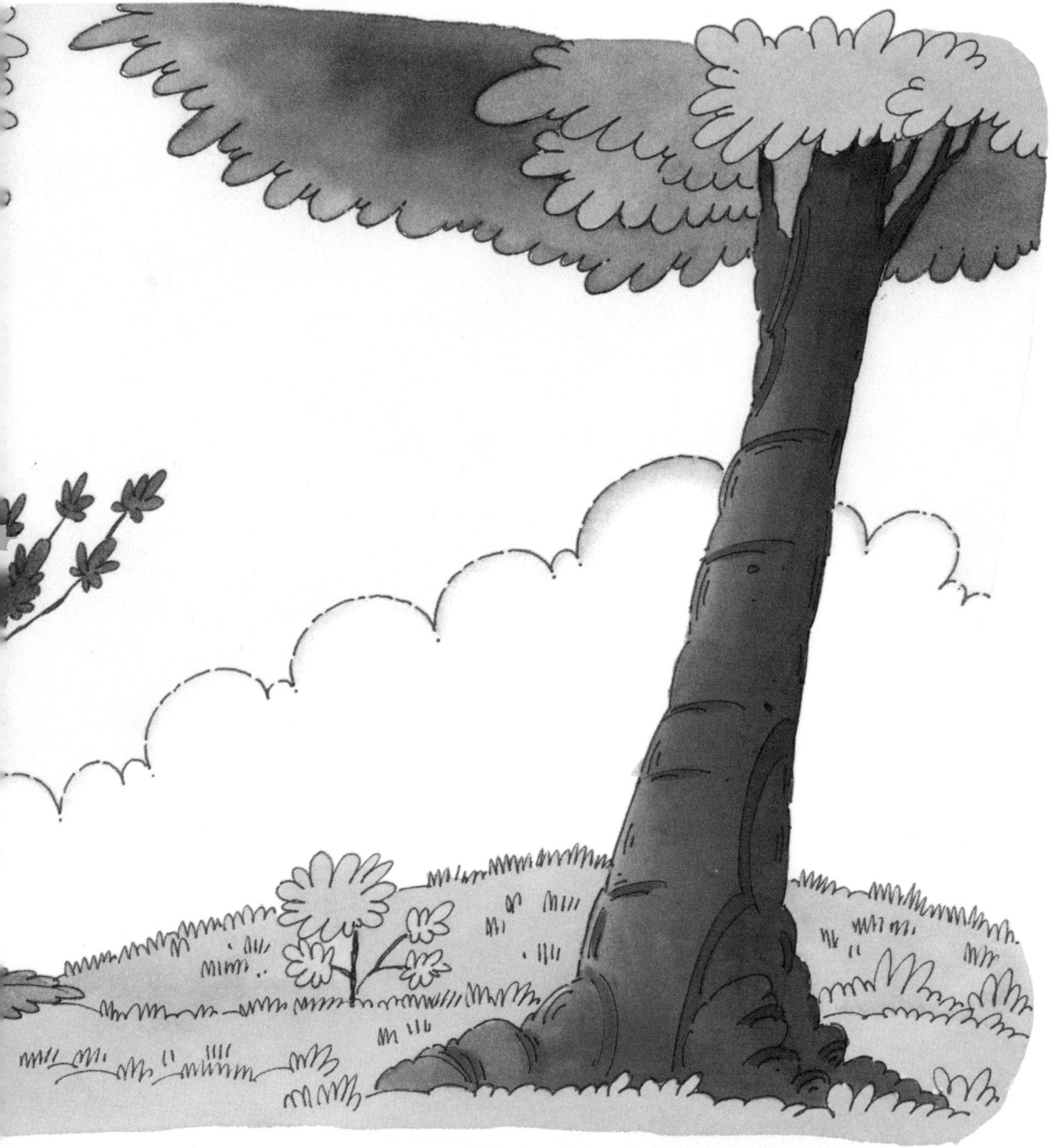

On the fourth day of creation, God made the sun, the moon, and the stars. God made **many** stars, but only a **few** planets. **Many** is the opposite of **few**.

God created all the fish in the sea and all the birds of the air on the fifth day.

He made **hard** shark teeth and **soft** sparrow feathers. **Hard** and **soft** are different. They are opposites.

On the sixth day, God made all kinds of animals.
He made **big** elephants and **little** mice. **Big** and **little** are
opposites.

God made **rough** rhinoceros skin
and **smooth** seal skin. **Rough** and
smooth are opposites.

God made the first **man**, Adam, and the first **woman**, Eve. **Man** and **woman** are opposites.

God makes all kinds of people. Some are **girls** and some are **boys**. Some are **tall** and some are **short**. Some have **black** hair and some have **white** hair.

Girls and **boys**, **tall** and **short**,
black and **white** are all opposites.

God loves you, just the way you are.

God, Thank You for creating the world.
Thank You for making opposites. I think You
had a very busy week!